*The Novelty of Effective
Leadership From
the Front Porch*

The Novelty of Effective Leadership From the Front Porch

Luv Alston

authorHOUSE®

AuthorHouse™
1663 Liberty Drive
Bloomington, IN 47403
www.authorhouse.com
Phone: 1-800-839-8640

First published by AuthorHouse 04/26/2011

ISBN: 978-1-4567-6449-4 (sc)
ISBN: 978-1-4567-6450-0 (ebk)

Printed in the United States of America

Any people depicted in stock imagery provided by Thinkstock are models,
and such images are being used for illustrative purposes only.
Certain stock imagery © Thinkstock.

This book is printed on acid-free paper.

Contents

Dedication

This book is dedicated to Gary who brings the wisdom no matter where we are; and to all my family, friends and colleagues who have sat on the front porch with me to gain in wisdom, emotional intelligence, knowledge or just great humor, at least I think I'm funny. This is also dedicated to my grandmother "Mu," and my grandfather "Daddy;" whose front porch I have some of my first and fondest memories. Mu and Daddy's front porch is also where I learned the foundation of the wisdom that I have built upon in life and the corporate world.

This is also dedicated to those Sistahs who raised a nation of Americans with a wise continence, a loving heart, a warm embrace and a rod.

Forward

by
Regina Friedman

Ahhh sitting on a front porch . . . ever since I was a child this vision evokes serenity and bliss . . . wouldn't it be wonderful if you and your staff and/or colleagues could feel this way in the work place? In most cases it is something one rarely feels as a stressed out manager or administrator. I think it is a wonderful scenario for this book on effective leadership given in a conversational format. I have immensely enjoyed these types of conversations with Luv who is a dear friend and colleague. She offers such articulate intelligence on this and many other subjects she has studied as she is able to speak her truth from the heart.

When I think about being effective in the world I know the truest actions come from my heart. Like Luv, I am also a manager and a motivational trainer and in every one of my speaking engagements I speak of the need for self connection . . . a relationship with oneself in order to be effective with all other relationships in life. For how can you be truly present with another if you are not in tune with taking care of your own mind/body/spirit? The human experience is all about finding ways to connect within and in doing so, with one another. Taking daily care and replenishing one self, so that you don't burn out, is the only way to succeed and will lead you on the path of effective leadership.

Effective leaders lead simply by modeling kind and loving behavior; and actually taking the time to connect to themselves and others in this way. For it has been said that we remember more how we *feel* when we are with another versus what activities we do with them. I try to keep this in mind with all my relationships and as I interact in my community. This same action is at the core of what Luv is expressing in this book regarding the novelty of effective leadership in the work place.

Throughout the book Luv addresses the important concepts that support kindness in leadership for example, individualized meetings, encouraging talent of others, emotional intelligence, choosing to change and building sustainable relationships. Being resilient to maintain the integrity of who you are in spite of differences is one of the greater challenges. Luv speaks openly and honestly accepting the truth about herself (the good and the bad) which supports self awareness so that she can connect with others and respond in a healthy way (or acknowledge when she did not respond appropriately so that she can address this and move on as well).

It is vital as a leader to acknowledge when it's all about feeling you are right, while realizing at the same time so does your staff member, boss or colleague, this is an important first step to begin to slow down and listen. You may consider living by the philosophy to "Seek first to understand then to be understood" which is one of Stephen R. Covey's "7 Habits of Highly Effective People". Luv explains the only real change you can affect is how you respond to others; which depends on how open and present you are with them.

This may have a trickle affect, as it can cause their response to change too, however you do not have any control over whether that happens or not.

Luv shares stories that support change and the impact on the ability of staff to do their jobs effectively when they feel they are respected, seen and heard as an individual. In the end I feel this brings Luv's point of being an effective leader home to where it belongs in one's heart.

I know that Luv and I hope by reading this book you feel as empowered as we do, to be an effective leader and ambassador of change where you make solid connections and support both yourself and staff/colleagues. For the only thing that we can count on in life is that it is forever changing. This knowledge also provides the freedom to know each day you can strive to be a better person, one who leads and makes connections through kind heartfelt actions. I am confident that you will find key concepts/phrases and thoughts to reflect on as you sit on your own front porch, which incidentally can be wherever you feel peaceful in your home etc. Luv wouldn't want it any other way. Peace

Preface

We are sitting on the front porch. Isn't Regina awesome? I know, I am blessed to have Regina as a friend and sister-friend. So come on up the steps and find a chair, we have plenty of room. Yes, and welcome. I am as happy to have you join us as I am hopeful. I have to tell you that there is something magical and awesome about the wisdom of that open air room. It is surrounded by the sounds of children playing, birds singing in the trees and cats teasing dogs until they bark themselves silly. However, it is the wisdom and understanding gained about life and corporate life that is truly amazing. Now, I would like to tell you that people come from all over, or I'm the front porch guru for leadership to others, but it is not true, I learn just as much as I have ever taught anyone from the front porch and abroad. Nevertheless, I will try to give you some usable portion of what I have come to know in easy lessons that you can use immediately as a manager in the workplace to become an effective leader.

Have a seat and join our discourse with regard to some leadership theory that you will hopefully be able to put into daily practice. That's right, since we are talking from the front porch, you will please excuse me when I have to take a break to get some tea or catch a good breeze. Let me know if you need anything. I hope that you will also forgive that I did not have this book edited for correct grammar. I wanted you to hear me as I speak in the most natural way of communication for me. This way we can have a frank conversation. So feel welcome to talk with me and write notes in and on the Front Porch.

The first thing I should do is establish my "street cred." So I will, as it seems curiously important to the people within the working world. I have been an RN for over 20 years, you know since Jesus was a CEO. I also have a BA from Indiana University. I minored in psychology and organizational behavior coursework. This is where I first heard about and dove deep into emotional intelligence. My main focus was to become a student of my own behaviors and hopefully evolve from dragging my emotional knuckles to being an upright biped. I have worked in the corporate world for nearly 30 years and am a part of a management team. More importantly, I am a leader and a dedicated front porcher.

I am also an author of two, so far, fantasy books: Book One and Book Two of Seven. I know, shameless plug. The second of which was a finalist for Foreword Magazine's book of the year. Yes, I am just a little proud of myself and the book writing thing is important to how I became an effective leader. Writing fantasy books requires a tremendous amount and diversity of study in a wide range of subjects. It is quite similar to what you should do as a daily part of your work to becoming a good leader and then a great leader. I have also written and conducted cultural diversity and emotional intelligence in workplace trainings. I am a presenter with over 15 years experience.

No matter where I go, I think I have something written on me, people talk to me about what is going on with them within their organizations. I kid you not; I was at the pool, my only sanctuary, besides the front porch, to watch my daughter during swim lessons. I bring out my chair; sit at the side of the olympic size pool off to myself. I sit away from all of the other parents and it never fails that someone comes up to me to tell me about their problems with the hope that I can solve them for them. I don't know how or why but I often do solve problems. I just can't seem to help myself, it's like a puzzle, but I seriously I don't use pixy dust nor do I wave a magic wand.

I tell people this thing called the truth and I am big believer in this other thing called honesty. Usually, that truth involves explaining to them that their problems are rooted in their choices and behaviors. I know, I don't like to hear it either, but it's true. As adults we make choices that affect our lives and those around us. We can choose to be a leader, a follower, a victim, a manager or a jackass, but whatever, it is a choice. Apparently, you are choosing to be an effective leader. Okay, I am here for you. So let's get started. I will try to make this as painless as possible, though I can't make any promises. I do want this book to be easy to use. Thus, the chapters are, for the most part, short with a word or more on the why of an action or document.

Chapter One

Wisdom and Effective Leadership

Wisdom is a main ingredient of effective leadership. There are books that will tell you that leadership is fundamentally one thing: The ability to influence others. This is true to a degree, but there are layers of wisdom, a combination of knowledge and experience, and a few other ingredients that go into building an effective leader. The word leadership is similar to, in its function, the word reinforcement; there are positive and negative choices to both. Just like you can use positive stimuli to encourage behavior to be repeated, you can also use negative stimuli to encourage behavior to be repeated. In fact, though the theories are sound on using positive reinforcement rather than negative, people still tend to beat a dead horse.

Leadership is the same way. You can choose to become a leader that influences others to be self serving to a person, sex, institution, organization, country, race, religion etc., or you can choose to be a leader that influences others to do good and excellent works for other people despite the fact that an individual or a group is not a part of your "group." Therefore, the question is not whether you can become a leader, because you can fundamentally learn the skills required to influence others. The question is more about what type of leader you will choose to be.

I hope you want to be a world class leader. I hope that you choose positive, effective leadership rather than negative leadership, but the choice, of course, is your own. In any case, I want to share with you something about being a manager, which is not exactly, in and of itself, synonymous with effective leadership while you think about which type of leader you want to be. A manager is a person who has organizational authority to tell others what to do. This person usually has a badge with a title.

It has been my experience that good managers understand the projects that need to be managed. They can often be "task oriented," rather than "people oriented." They can be, but generally are not, creative and have little or no visionary abilities. They usually ensure projects get done and tasks are on time. Leaders love them, because they will pay attention to little details and encourage forward movement in the right direction. They are by and large smart and effective. Many are also very "political," (which can, at times, be synonymous with organizational bully {OB}). They seem to say yes no matter the job. We can tell you from the front porch that "yes" people are a dime a dozen. It takes great skills to stand up to your boss or organization when you are passionate about something when everyone else remains complicit.

Ineffective manager's behaviors are similar to good managers except an ineffective manager is lost when they do not understand the task or the moving parts to a project. A good manager can quickly become an ineffective manager given the circumstances. Since they are not generally people persons and lack leadership skills, they tend to use coercion to get tasks accomplished through others or end up doing the tasks themselves when their direct reports (staff) drop off fed up. Many managers, good or ineffective, have very little to no ability to influence others without pulling rank. Most good managers learn how to encourage or motivate others, while many ineffective managers leave that to the leaders in a given organization or institution.

This then, becomes the distinction between ineffective managers, effective managers, good leaders and great leaders. An ineffective manager does not meet deadlines and may or may not deliver favorable results on a consistent basis. Sometimes this happens due to mistakes, bad choices and or lack of training. An effective manager meets both deadlines and consistently provides positive project outcomes. Some managers accomplish project management by means of leadership (good managers) and some do so by bullying (ineffective managers).

Good, effective leaders on the other hand:

1. Have the ability to influence others; they give trust and work to gain the trust of others by being self-aware, a student of their and others' behaviors, listen; give feedback and recommendations in a respectful and dignified manner.
2. Study leadership, history, current events and relationship building/ people and encourage others to grow both personally and professionally.
3. Are risk takers, yet display wisdom and understanding.
4. Are visionary and are big picture thinkers.
5. Are creative.

6. Open to diverse lines of thinking, displaying consistently evolving emotional intelligence (this distinguishes them from bad leaders).

7. Hold themselves, as well as others accountable (this distinguishes them from bad leaders). They display a high degree of integrity. They disciple, rather than punish.

8. Take responsibility for ill results, but share credit or give credit fully to others for positive results (this distinguishes them from bad leaders)

9. People would willingly follow them whether the leader had any authority or not as they tend to engender trust.

10. They choose the right people who are already passionate and motivated to do the excellent thing. They also help the wrong people for a job decide to find the right job for them.

Great leaders are good leaders and are necessarily good project managers. First we have to be good, effective leader.

Good managers do have their place and there are some good managers who are also excellent, great leaders, but this animal is rare, as the manager is like the left side of our brain and a good leader is like the right side of our brain. This is why you see both in organizations. Good and or great leadership are choices. You can choose, then, to be a manager who studies your company's policies, standards and procedures to effectively manage projects. You can also choose to trust the experts on the teams you support to, with the proper procedural training, handle the moving parts of larger projects. Further, you can choose to study leadership, your behaviors and the behaviors of others to take corrective actions to support your staff.

My friend Pammy said something one day when we were on the front porch, "a badge only gives you literal access to a building. That has nothing to do with forming good relationships and being able to do a good enough job at the work or kissing a . . . to stay there." Too true and lesson learned.

We have a simple tool that we use on the front porch to find out whether you are an effective leader. You have to be ready to hear the truth before you do this so be warned. When you feel you can handle it, send out the following anonymous survey to all the staff you support on your company's organizational chart. All staff, not just your friends.

Hint: If people are doing what you say, but they mark no on the survey and therefore they would not follow you if your organization did not make them do so because of your position; it's because you have a badge. If they mark yes, it's because they would view as a leader no matter your position.

Tool: Manager vs Leader Survey

If I did not have my current position and I worked with you instead of above you, would you follow me? Yes_____ No___

Chapter Two

Individualized One to One

Now that we know what it means to be a manger and leader, it's time to share more tools with you that will help you become a good leader and encourage others to follow you. There are just a few tools and they are simple in nature. What is not so simple is the behavior changes required for you to go about building and sustaining trusting relationships. Consequently, throughout the next few chapters we will be discussing that the way to change other people is by changing the only thing you really have control over, yourself, your actions, reactions and behaviors.

You are welcome to use the tools as they are or tweak them as you see fit. I suggest you use them first and to find out what may work better for you and your group.

The first tool is the Individual One to One Agenda. We discussed useful explanations as to how to best use the tools, but first I will tell you how I have seen versions of this used in most organizations. Usually, organizations work from the top down. There is a chain of command. A "leader," who sets the vision, a director to direct the vision, coordinators to coordinate the direction of the vision and supervisors to manage the people who actually do the work. In many organizations people have multiple roles. This may be why one to one's, when they occur, favor the agenda of the supervisor rather than the staff the supervisor supports.

If there is someone up top who cares to have one to one meetings with their subordinates, it is usually to touch base to find out where the subordinate is on a project or task or to tell them of impending projects and tasks that need to be done. This may also be the time for the supervisor to tell the subordinate what he/she did can improve upon. This is important to add to a one to one, but in the suggestions and other portions. The first item to be addressed is the needs of the staff from their perspective.

Management often reverses the tool. The agenda does help the manager and often leaves the staff without a voice. Remember those considered subordinate may have information to share that would be a benefit to the project or manager. Again, the "other" within the tool is designated to ask if the subordinate has anything to add or do they really want to waste the time of their supervisor when there are so many tasks to complete. We chose to change this tool to fit the needs of the supervisor and the staff the supervisor supports. It is a radical change and in the estimation of the front porchers, that's us, a necessary one.

The one to one agenda consists of several simple questions adapted from one of my mentors in one of the required reading books at the end of this book. Organizational behaviorists suggest directly supervising no more than seven to nine people. Optimal is somewhere around six people under your direct supervision. Your directly supervised staff can supervise the same numbers successfully. We recommend keeping workgroups this size as well. Directly supervising small numbers of staff allows you to serve up to two hours a month for their individual one to ones. Yes, I said two hours. Smaller groups also encourage great collaborations and ease of norming within each team.

Just imagine if your boss came to you every month and asked you how you envision your job and if you could have anything to go about your job in an excellent manner, what would it be? Well, this is what we encourage you to do with your team in your individualized one to one. You may not be able to give them everything that they wish for, but your focus for the next few days between your duties at work and maintaining other relationships should be to find out how you can make at least the top one or two wishes that month come true. For instance, I found out in the one on one with my team that they wanted to change the logistics of how they did their work. I am a let's try it and see what happens kind of chick, so they did. They love it and they are twice as productive. Practice saying it with me, "okay, let's try it." We are known for our radical ideas as front porchers and for our rogue, out of the house (box) thinking. All we ask is that you give this tool a whirl. We must work to give all consumers of our services (our staff, bosses, other teams we support) including customers, an opportunity to participate in team discussions.

Within the two hours the one to one should include the following:

1. What is working or is successful for you?
2. What is not working or is unsuccessful for you?
3. What do you think we can do or should do to change what isn't working?

4. Other, this is for you to add any housekeeping items (i.e. new projects, adjustment to current projects, updates, timelines and work plans. You might also add some mentorship and information to grow on.

I like to think of myself as a female Willy Wonka. He wrote a song about it . . . "If you want to view paradise simply look around and view it, anything you want to do it . . . wanna change the world, there's nothing to it . . ." I am literally asking them what they think should happen with the job that they do every day. I want to know how they think I can make their jobs easier to complete. I want to know how well I am communicating or if there is more I can do to communicate better or more efficiently. I want to know what their ultimate dreams are for the job that they do. There's more, but you get it.

It is of high importance that one to ones are private and confidential, who said what is not to be shared without the express permission of the other group member. The only thing you can share with those above you are the requests made without telling who made them. Your job with the third portion is to try to make their dreams come true for their job. I know, nuts right? Can we get a "whoop, whoop," for your boss' adaptation to a one to one each month to find out from you what you would like to see happen to do your job excellently.

We realize the enormity of what we are suggesting. It's almost too much to take in. Many managers question how they are to implement such radical idealism when, "that is not how it goes around here." Too many express legitimate disappointment in their organization's leadership. There so many books on bad bosses. Maybe you are just coming to work for your check too. Front porchers understand. Most people run across the manager from the sixth ring of hell, horns and all.

Though dysfunctional behaviors tend to be a direct result of top leadership rolling down to management and staff, it needs to stop with us. We are accountable for our behaviors and the results of our behaviors. Consider when Kathy Lee Gifford was charged with running sweat shops that used child labor and her reactions. Consider the behaviors of the Enron organization.

Those of us who gain in organizational wisdom from the front porch need to work on building our emotional intelligence, leadership skills and human behavioral understanding. We want our teams to know that they are worthy of our daily esteem, regard and support. So, let's stop talking about it and be about the business of behaving in a manner that shows how much we believe in the front porch mantras.

Refuse to delight in the misery of organizationally mediocrity. Choose a different path. Many front porchers have firsthand knowledge of the ignorance and inhumanity, at times, with which leadership and management can treat staff. We can change entire organizational cultures by choosing to behave differently than the organizational norm as much of the bullying is inbred with hierarchical (top down) organizational cultures. It is easy to point fingers and recognize what "they" are doing however we must first be aware of our own behaviors. We can help organizations to encourage giving employees a voice and empower each member of the staff to do excellent work.

From personal experience, it is uplifting to see my team dancing in the parking lot, getting enormous amounts of work done grinning all the while. That's right, I said it, and they are highly productive because they are great people, who are great at what they do and they are highly motivated. I put in work to earn their high regard and trust. I ask for some hard things with crazy timelines and they deliver with excellence. All of this because I changed my behavior. All of this because I chose to study and practice good leadership skills.

Others use this concept and the tools with similar results. I don't know what to tell you; it just works, but you have got to change your behaviors and work from the successes of others not from their mistakes. There is something wrong with an organizational culture that punishes and dehumanizes staff for mistakes. What tends to happen is that people still make mistakes, but they will hide them, blame others or act as if they are clueless. This doesn't mean that you do not hold people accountable, you do, but the first thing is to be accountable yourself. Mistakes are a part of learning.

So when should you reprimand people or accept reprimand from your boss you might ask? Well, a onetime action (or mistake) is an incident that may occur again, if not acknowledged and learned from. A second or third of the same behavior could be a coincidence and clarity along with understanding should be a part of you conversation. A behavior that occurs four to five or more times is a behavioral pattern and requires, mentoring, coaching, retraining, monitoring and possible discipline. This does not count safety or incivility.

<u>Discipline</u> vs	<u>Punishment</u>
Relationship development (mentor, coach)	No relationship necessary
Clarity of rules and consequences	Judgmental, punishes with or without clarity of rules
If ___, Then___	?___, Then___
Values the person	Values or punishes results
Gives feedback	Hypercritical
Recognizes individual rights	Does not generally respect or value any rights other than own
Accepts the whole person and boundaries	Does not need to care about other's boundaries
Observes/ watches, listens to behaviors	Listen to other peoples' reports of behaviors
Says yes or no depending on situation	Says yes or no depending on the person
Practices being accountable admitting wrongs	Expects others to be accountable
Gives clear boundaries and accountability	
Considers situation, emotions and perceptions	Considers the person (like or dislike)
Listens for facts, and adherence to policies	Listen's to one side of situation, not necessarily the person being punished

Okay enough talk here is chapter two's tool.

Individualized One to One	
Meeting Date and Time	
Meeting Location	
Meeting Participant	
Participant	
What is working and Successful?	

AGENDA ITEM		Making it Work
1. What is not Working or is unsuccessful?		

Individualized One to One	
2. What do you think would work instead?	
a. How is your behaviour contributing to What's Working?	
b. What about your behaviour contributing to What's Not Working?	
c.	
d.	
e.	
f. Communication	
g.	
h. House Keeping	
3. How can I make this happen?	
a.	
b.	
c.	
d.	
e.	
f.	
g.	
4. Final decision	
5. Action planning	

Individualized One to One	
6. Meeting closure and review of next steps	
7. Other interests	
8. House Keeping	
9.	
10	

Notes:

Chapter Three

Accountability

Since we've broached the subject of accountability; there is an awesome tool we front porchers use to hold ourselves accountable for our responsibilities and others for their responsibilities. Simply, follow up whatever is said with an email. Keep a folder for each relationship be they an individual, group, institution or organization. Print out emails sent and or received and place them in the corresponding folder.

For example, I manage a service area that includes seven counties, close to 100 family child care homes and nearly 60 school sites. As you can imagine I cannot begin to remember everything I say to everyone that I built relationships with. So I invested in this wonderful creature called an Iphone and I follow-up what I say to people or conversations I have had with others with emails. Now there are other smart phones with tremendous applications like sticky notes, calendars and much more. I have a blackberry too, which I love. Whatever works for you. Emails are cheap, dated documentation. Emails keep us all, including and especially me, honest.

Okay, one other touchy little thing to say about accountability. Accountability and integrity applies to you first and foremost. You want to be known as a leader of your word, whether people like that word or not. Make a habit of righting wrongs, listening to feedback about your behaviors. Publically admit mistakes and bad choices. Take responsibility and say when you mess something up and should not have done something different. Remember to be a student of your own behaviors that lead to the bad choices. Also apologize when you inadvertently mistreat or approach others in a way that may hurt them.

Remember, a front porcher strives to be a good leader who works to be a great leader. A great leader takes responsibility for the results of projects of the teams lead by them. A great leader shares successes with the team. A great leader admits when they are wrong. A great leader takes responsibility for how their behaviors and decisions affect others. A great leader works to show others respect. A great leader is a good project manager too.

What we recommend you to do here is not easy. It requires strength of character and person, but a leader needs credibility to be able to influence others. Credibility requires integrity. Integrity means that what you say, and require of others, matches up to what you do on a daily basis. It tends to be human nature to see the wrongness of behaviors in everyone else and to blame our bad behaviors and choices on others and situations, but integrity demands that you take responsibility for the part that you play. Introduction of these concepts can change the way people react to you. Several managers and leaders I know became accountable and began using management by walking around. In interviews with their staff reveal that staff respond favorably to the changes in their leadership. Staff say far out stuff like,

"I would do anything that person asks of me." Okay, I am getting all tingly.

So back to what we discussed before the integrity speech. I do one to ones with from twenty to thirty people each month. Most of these are mini one to ones. The two hour one to ones are reserved for my direct reports (staff), coordinators and directors. To build capacity, I have trained others to duplicate this process with their direct reports, because they do the real work every day; while I ride around making sure that they have what they need to accomplish that work. It's awesome doing magic. Okay, I may have stretched the truth a bit. It is not exactly magic, in the world of organizational behavior it's called Management by walking around (MBWA). MBWA leads us to our next front porch topic.

Chapter Four
Magic (MBWA)

I enjoyed responsibility for service area that stretched from the valley in California to the California coast. I was promoted to this responsibility in April of my first year, by mid-July I was responsible to answer review questions and take the feds out to the diverse areas our company covered. I had three months to build sustainable relationships, provide monitoring, training and technical assistance for all of my areas. Did I mention that I had no direct reports (staff) until July? Did I mention that our workgroup pulled off a Review without findings? How did I do it? Well, that is what the reviewers asked. They also noticed that no matter where I took them, people actually acted as if they really knew me. First, I built sustainable relationships by taking my show on the road five days a week. Next I worked with an awesome team of program area experts, though not in my particular area, remain exceedingly supportive. Last our work group had a leader that allowed us to do our jobs. We produced work plans and documentation of quality assurance monthly for her, but she extended us trust. As evidenced by her behavior, she believed that as the experts in each of our areas, we would try to make the right calls.

Each of the areas we took the review team to had anywhere from seven to twenty line staff that worked with our diverse program areas. My job required that I work with coordinators and directors. Beyond that everything that could go wrong just about did. People came up missing in action (MIA), due to normal human stuff like having babies or being ill. To top it off my boss was on her way out. What saved the day? The magic of management by walking around (MBWA).

It wasn't an illusion, the staff did and do know me and I them. I have since trained others to duplicate this same success. Our team has grown and they live by the same code and core values that guide us here on the front porch. People are happy to see them come even though their job is fundamentally to monitor and check for quality. As front porchers themselves, they understand that monitoring for quality assurance begins with monitoring how well they monitor themselves. It also means that support be primary to the diverse teams being monitored. Any monitoring must begin with detailed look for system errors. Then monitoring must search for group and individual understanding and mentorship. Once the system is checked, training and technical assistance is received and then the monitor looks for individual issues.

You may work for a different company and what you oversee maybe the production of bagels. If the bagels are coming out looking like sliced bread as the supervisor your job is not to point fingers. Front porchers don't look at individuals until we have examined the system, procedures, clarification of procedures and whether training is not only done, but understood by each person held accountable. Then we make plans to counter each area examined depending on the findings. Further, going out to work sites, picking up a broom as a leader, lending a hand to staff as management, not only helps staff, but allows for ultimate understanding of the staff and the work being done.

We believe in mass trainings and one on one mentoring. In the mentoring phase, the idea is to work with the individual team members to ensure that each understands what is required according to the standards and procedures. Going around checking in on members of the team provides management a basis for building and sustaining relationships. MBWA also allows for an understanding of team needs, strengths and system errors.

Take your or any organizational chart, at least 80-90% have the executives on top, management in the middle and service on the bottom. When I work with a company, I ask for their chart and then invert it. The most important part of any company is the customer. One of the most important customers of the leadership of any organization is the staff.

A few people tell me that their staff should just know what to do and that as a supervisor no one should have to babysit another adult. Alas all of that tis true, to a degree. However, if no one ever teaches the management and leadership how to support their people, because a lot of what I do is mentoring other supervisors and my team too, then who will support those who provide customer service.

Therefore, the most important staff is actually three fold: the line-staff (those who provide direct customer services), the techies and the secretaries. Oh yeah, I don't want to forget the oompa loompas who keep our world functioning and clean, the maintenance and housekeeping teams. Although, I don't think our oompa loompas have the awesome singing voices of the originals, not that fake new Tim Burton thing.

You may quite possibly receive flak for this behavior from your boss at first, but remember we are working to turn most leadership to the front porch motif. Remember, not every leader knows about front porchers, but I'm not bitter. I am willing to transform leadership one person at a time.

As a supervisor or manager or leader, part of your job requires you to monitor, encourage and ensure that staff is prepared to do the job they were hired to do. I am sure I have seen that "management" policy over and over again at diverse corporations. It seems that only new employees read it and management only dusts it off and pulls it out to impress guests.

There is a story of a nice woman who was overwhelmed by her job as a supervisor; in fact I meet a lot of people who feel this way. They were promoted due to their ability to manage projects. The thought process being that if you can do one thing well, then you do ten other things as well and teach others how you did the first thing so that they too can duplicate the process.

The problem with this scenario is that a good manager is only as good as their understanding of a given project, when given processes they do not understand or are too massive to do alone then they must become instant leaders. Contrary to what you may have heard all of these years the sun does not rise in the east and set in the west, um the earth revolves around the sun; and people are not generally born leaders, but they can learn the skills if they are willing to work on their own behavior. I know that I mentioned this before, but . . . anyway back to my story.

So, this nice woman was promoted, not oriented to her new position through any type of mentorship. Her temperament was slow to warm and she was somewhat shy. She also did not want her boss or director to think that she did not know what to do. She had not gone over her job description since she took the job and it had changed. The entire organization changed from supporting staff to a huge beast that no longer knew the names of individuals. She was just another person lost in the fray. She could not see that she was repeating the same behavior with her teams that was being done to her by those above her.

What would you do in this scenario? Have you ever found yourself in this position? The first thing we have to remember is not to do my second favorite thing, blame. I know it's hard and I so love being right too, but we want an equitable solution. So the answer is to investigate the system. I and a colleague go in, investigate the systems in place and develop relationships. Then we work to support teams, you know emails, one to ones, mentoring. We also help people to recognize their own complicity in a given situation.

It was not easy to hear that we each need to be accountable for our behaviors and responsible for the results of those behaviors. Therefore my colleagues and I habitually mirror each other. We train others on relationship development with staff by using magic. Did you forget about MBWA already? The heroine of our story began making that a part of her routine for each week. She went from not visiting the team at all, and waiting for them to call her with issues, to visiting and doing one on ones three or more times per week. It changed the outcome of the job. She was no longer stretched beyond imagining, because she had the support of the team she gave support to. Truly, her behavior changed from putting out fires to preventing them. Wow, I am getting all misty eyed just thinking about it.

I go out of my way to ensure that I support and treat special those groups who do the real work. I encourage you to rethink your organizational chart and consider what I am saying here. It has become a natural inclination of ours to kiss up to the top portion of an organization, while those below us on the chart get paid the least to do the most heavy lifting. It takes me back to that scene in Charlie and the Chocolate Factory when that one girl, Faruza's, father, had an army of women in his company opening up thousands of candy bars to find his little brat the golden ticket. Does anyone even remember what the lady who found it looks like? I do. Many companies still have not let go of that industrial age mindset. I encourage you to do so.

Hey, I like the candy man; he was a leader after my own heart. We are in a war with virmicious cannids, I suggest you pony up.

Chapter Five

Tool: Work Plans

One of the tools that can help keep you and your team on track is a project or work plan. People often do not want to hear that this will be one more thing that they have to do, but what is that old saying 'failing to plan is planning to fail.' Two of my fellow front porchers create these awesome work plans that truly put me to shame. My little plans are not so elaborate, but functional nonetheless. You can tweak this so that it works for you since I do not have the monopoly on work or project plans. I usually do one every three months, however you may do them as often as you need or wish, but quarterly, at the least is a must.

Work Plan

Objectives *(What are the overall goals of the task or projects to be completed)*
Budget *(What will it cost, including work hours, travel, supplies, etc.)*
Risk Assessment *(What or who may hinder task completion)*

Task 1	Person(s) Accountable for Completion	Additional Information, Input, Supplies or Support Needed	Estimated Completion Date	Actual Completion Date
Task 2				
Task 3				

Notes:

Chapter Six

Organizations Urban Legends Clearing Up Communication with Emotional Intelligence

Emotional intelligence (EI), a concept developed by Daniel Goleman, is more often whispered about in many organizations, with a top down organizational chart, than used. Emotional Intelligence is a four pronged process that I have added a fifth and ultimate piece to called leadership. It has been my experience that if someone can master the first four elements of EI, then they are well on their way to becoming a positive and progressive leader.

That sounds easy you say? Kinda, and yet not. It requires each person to take responsibility for the part they play in their relationships with others. For example there are three things that are a part of my temperament. First, I love to be right. Second, I love to blame. Third and this is important if you ever invite me to come speak at your organization, I love cake. Now, if I get to have all of three things in one day, it's an awesome day.

I learned this about myself during my journey to develop my own emotional intelligence. I learned some other things too about how my behaviors come across to others. The three issues with my temperament were vital for me to get about myself in order to make an evolutionary change in my behavior. It's been my experience that humans tend to believe our environment affects us. Tis true to a degree, however we also affect our environment.

I know, shocking right? So, though I love to be right, there is a problem in that the other person(s) must either agree with me or they are wrong. Being right leaves no room for diverse opinion. I also love to blame, however the problem with that is I don't take responsibility for my behavior and that's not okay. And cake, though scrumptious has single-handedly caused me to have ginormous hips, high blood pressure and off the chart cholesterol. See, now I am even blaming cake for my eating it. I guess I have more work to do.

Developing a high EI takes years in some cases. It is an ongoing cycle of the study self-behavior, learning to control emotions and bad behaviors, not that you have any, and daily reading. EI involves becoming aware and empathetic to the emotions of others and then learning how to have clear communication and feedback in order to ensure that the emotions of others are working for their own benefit and that of the project at hand. Oh did I mention that I am a recovering drama junkie too? Between attending my twelve step program for blaming, drama junkie and weight watchers, I barely have time to watch the Housewives and Burn Notice. 'Hi, I am Luv and I am a drama junkie . . .'Just practicing for next week's meeting.

If we can reach a point through the study of our behaviors, and the behaviors of others and we can learn to communicate with the best interest of the other person in mind . . . Wow just imagine? I just love it when someone told someone, who told my cousin, who said to my sister that we should be doing this task or that project that way, and the organizational policies do not say any of what we know to be oral tradition. These are organizational urban legends and it must be stopped or at least discussed. Study of written policies, procedures and standards helps to clear that away so everyone has clarity of their roles, the roles of others and how and why of the tasks to be completed.

Chapter Seven

Work Group Meetings vs Staff Meetings

Surely staff meetings have their place on the seventh ring of hell; front porchers prefer, in a utopian organization to use them during a special occasion, such as, delivery of great company news in person and in mass. Staff meetings, by their nature, tend to be cold and sterile. They are usually the agenda of one person. We prefer work group meetings. Work group meetings allow each member of the team the opportunity to add to the agenda, share ideas and offer feedback.

A friend told me that she learned to write "shh . . ." at the top of the agenda given at the staff meeting she attends with her boss. She does this, sadly, to remind herself not to say anything or question her boss. I know of many other people in diverse organizations who feel the same about their staff meetings. It just seems a time in which people are given a list of what they better do, then a list of what better not happen again and then a stern, "are there any questions?" Which really is code for "who dares question their sovereign lord?"

To add injury to insult, these meetings go on for two, four, sometimes eight hours. I know how these meetings feel as I have fought the demons back in my own head at staff meetings, attended over the years, who were whispering . . . "please dear God send me back to hell where the moaning of the damned actually makes sense." Sorry, my fantasy writing coming out again.

Honestly, two of the beings whispering to me aren't demons, but my own personal angels, and both are actually friends of mine, Hilda and Tigger. Both of them sit on the front porch with thirty years of corporate knowledge between them. They are two of the funniest women you ever want to meet. These two are brilliant in their assessments and they can mumble with a smile on their faces the entire time we are in these meetings. There is nothing like having trusted people you can let down your hair with and they hold you accountable at the same time as a part of your tribe, but I digress.

These two and my friend Regina are mirrors for me and help me see the follow of my own poor behaviors. I can admit that I have given these very same staff meetings without thought to the needs of my team as I was only pushing my agenda. All of them will tell me when I am being inconsiderate to the needs of others, rambling or inappropriately venting. We all need mirrors like my friends on the front porch.

As a result of recognizing my behavior and how it feels to be on the receiving end, a front porch secret we use involves the encouragement of team members to add to work group agendas. Allow them to choose the date and place to meet. As a supervisor, you can add housekeeping stuff to the agenda too and be there to clarify issues. However, each meeting should encourage group participation, feedback and diverse meeting facilitators. I know, so radical.

Who knows what would happen if this got out. People might feel empowered in their job. They might even start to like coming to work. What next, ruling the world? Wouldn't it be nice to manage a cooperative, gleeful team in an otherwise Dilbert type work environment? When your company has to make it mandatory that staff attend group functions that are supposed to increase morale, and staff are coming up with every excuse not to go, you know you are not working in the most enlightened environment.

How can you change an entire organization, you ask? One person at a time and one meeting at a time. Seriously, when I have to go to mandatory functions I want cake people, cake, oh and pepsi.

Chapter Eight

Singing Praises

It has been found in behavioral studies that while people remember the negative and "constructive," criticism they are told, they evolve and change behaviors much more often when the reinforcement is positive. If your workplace does not have a staff recognition system embedded within, then you should create one of your own. People need to feel good about what they do to motivate them to repeat and improve upon behaviors.

At least four times per year, usually more, look for reasons to recognize successes in a public fashion. Tell anyone who will listen that you have a phenomenal team. More importantly, make sure your team knows how much you delight in their excellent work.

One job I had has hero awards. I give them to people on other teams, as well as my team. I also give them to people I don't necessarily like. This is important. You won't like or get along with everyone you work for, with or support, but you do, but fairness and as impartiality are crucial to great leadership. Therefore, recognition for a job well done should not be based on whether you like the person or not, but on awesome accomplishments. On the inverse, people that you like should be held accountable for their work too. No favorites on the front porch, we are honest and forthright, especially with those closest to us, because we care.

The underlying secret to helping your team, and other colleagues, feel appreciated for a success requires genuine, humble behaviors. Now I do what I call WOW catching. The original concept is from one of my heroes Tony Hsieh., the CEO of Zappos. He discusses WOW customer service in his book *Delivering Happiness*. I do what I call WOW awards because I believe that great customer service begins with me being a servant leader who is accountable and responsible for results. I develop and sustain relationships. I am clear about boundaries and respect the boundaries of others. I also believe that you work with people to close gaps behind closed doors and you celebrate, even the most minor success loudly so that everyone can hear it.

Just a note, please don't give with one hand and bash and or gossip with the other. None of this, 'I like what you did but . . . Recognition should be kept separate from discussions of accountability except for during an evaluation.

Oh and a word about negative feedback on evaluations and positive feedback for that matter; both should be grounded in the policies and procedures executed, not based on your personal opinion good, bad or indifferent of the person. We work with all types of people and it is imperative that we be willing to listen to and investigate all sides of a story. Nothing is worse than being maligned by someone and never having your side or both of your sides heard. I am sure it has happened to you before, please don't turn around and do to others what never felt good when it was done to you.

Tool: Recognition

Star Recognition

has set the gold standard. This is in recognition of your quality work and excellent support.

Chapter Nine

The Case for Workplace, and Other Place Assholes

This may sound nuts, and it may be. I want to attempt to make the case for the necessity of workplace, and other place, assholes. This is in no way meant to hype assholes or asshole behavior. This chapter is simply to make an argument by giving a conclusion and supporting it with premises for why we experience so many of them especially in leadership positions in the workplace. Oh, for those of you who may be sensitive to the word asshole, we will also call them OBs, (Organizational Bullies).

There is a theory that suggests that they exist and their behavior is, not only tolerated, but is encouraged, as they may be the best at the details of project management. They are usually smart people and many times are well educated. They are usually quite literal when the administration above them gives them a license to "do whatever it takes to complete or undermine a project." Usually, the actions they take betray little integrity and a lack of understanding or ability to care for subordinates that are too heterozygous either in their look, creativity, ability, skills, mental process and fit-in-ability.

You should know, if you have not witnessed it already that the asshole, sorry, OB will not only throw people under the bus, but will drive the bus and then back up over their target. Further, they are willing to do what the administration or powers above them are unwilling to; they can heartlessly pick targets to bully to advance both their individual agendas while kissing the asses above them at the same time. They accomplish the dirty work.

Okay, I hear you. You still disagree with my argument. Believe me; I knew it would not be easy to convince you. You are right to question why any organization, in this day and time, would hire people and watch them destroy morale and dehumanize others. In other words, why would a management team get with and knowingly encourage such behavior, even promoting the offender to higher positions within the organization. All the while, these organizations write nifty core values and mission statements that possess a jingle like quality of lip service in the name of caring and the valuing of others. When in reality little to none of that is practiced. Also, there are many books on the subject of workplace bullying, a few on your reading list, if you wish to delve deeper and read up on the many studies completed by various writers.

For now, let's go back a ways and let me introduce you to some information I studied many years ago while conducting research for my other books. I am using the Bible as a reference, not to offend Christians or believers, but to make the case for OBs in the workplace. Just bear with me. You may not agree, but I am going to go there anyway.

<u>Job 1</u>

CHAPTER 1

"**1** <u>There was a man in the land of Uz, whose name *was*</u> <u>Job; and that man was perfect and upright, and one that</u> <u>feared God, and eschewed evil."</u>

Wait, I just want to say that by all accounts Job was upstanding and a good, God fearing man. He worshiped the right way and raised his family the right way. He was wen and aware of his behaviors. He was a good husband, father and provider and yet he became a target for workplace bullying. Maybe Job was annoying in his goodness, and we know that he was irritatingly loyal, and oozed with integrity. If we look at it from the asshole, sorry I did it again, OB perspective, we can see what may have made Job a target. Okay, back to our Job story . . .

"**6** <u>Now there was a day when the sons of God came to</u> <u>present themselves before the LORD, and Satan came also</u> <u>among them. 7 And the LORD said unto Satan, Whence</u> <u>comest thou? Then Satan answered the LORD, and said,</u> <u>From going to and fro in the earth, and from walking up</u> <u>and down in it. **8** And the LORD said unto Satan, Hast</u> <u>thou considered my servant Job, that *there is* none like him</u> <u>in the earth, a perfect and an upright man, one that feareth</u> <u>God, and escheweth evil?"</u>

This also begs us to look at why Satan was even a part of the staff meetings in heaven to begin with. So, I believe in clarifying and I have a pretty awesome relationship with God so hold on while I, heathen that I am, put this question to the Almighty. 'I mean come on God, Satan, the ultimate asshole picking on Job, is that really fair?'

No offense, but God being all knowing had to see that Satan would pull out all of the stops in his quest to be top

OB. He was tossed out for trying to take over heaven and yet there he was having a regular conversation with God and questioning God's favor of Job. God, not only allows this, but does not seem in the least offended. In fact, God is complicit in the actions taken against Job. Alright, alright on with the story . . .

9 Then Satan answered the LORD, and said, Doth Job fear God for nought? **10** Hast not thou made an hedge about him, and about his house, and about all that he hath on every side? thou hast blessed the work of his hands, and his substance is increased in the land. **11** But put forth thine hand now, and touch all that he hath, and he will curse thee to thy face. **12** And the LORD said unto Satan, Behold, all that he hath *is* in thy power; only upon himself put not forth thine hand. So Satan went forth from the presence of the LORD.

Verses 13-8 states that, among other things, Satan destroyed Job's home, killed his business, oh yeah, killed all of his children and left him the comfort of a nagging and somewhat bitter wife. I guess I would be nagging and bitter too after all of that. I know, I just can't take it. Now, this was bullying at its organizational best. I won't even read you the part where later, closer to the end of the story, Job questions God and God was all, "who are you to question me?" Yet, Satan gets to question and bully.

20 "Then Job arose, and rent his mantle, and shaved his head, and fell down upon the ground, and worshipped, **21** And said, Naked came I out of my mother's womb, and naked shall I return thither: the LORD gave, and the LORD hath taken away; blessed be the name of the LORD. **22** In all this Job sinned not, nor charged God foolishly.

In chapter two Satan is at the next staff meeting in heaven and this time he asks God if he can attack Job's body. God admits once more that Job is the perfect man and gives Satan the go ahead to attack Job.

"**7** So went Satan forth from the presence of the LORD, and smote Job with sore boils from the sole of his foot unto his crown."

There are several moral lessons here. Now, I am not saying that if God did it, then it should be okay for organizations to send Satan, or some other OB out on a mission to target, bully and torture people. I am simply saying that maybe God just did not like Job for some reason. Maybe God wanted to prove to Satan the resiliency of humans and that though humans are fallible and life is unfair, they can choose to behave right. Maybe God did not want to be seen as the bad guy, but whatever God's reasoning, he used Satan to bully Job. I have seen organizations not only allow, but encourage a much more insidious form of bullying.

Here is what I know about work place bullies, (OB): They choose targets that are in some way vulnerable to attacks and pettiness. Just like in the case of Job, the target may be attacked because the OB perceives them as a threat. It may be that the person is targeted because they are shy, different, unwilling or unable to defend themselves. It could be that the OB has in some unknown way been slighted by the target or the target simply does not fit in with the mean girls' behaviors (even men can be mean girls). It could be that the target is well liked and respected by others thereby engendering the enmity of the OB. It could be that the target looks or seems too different from the OB.

There a number of reasons why the OB may target someone to bully, but what is clear is that it is never fair or impartial and it almost always centers itself around personal attacks rather than feedback on actual and meaningful job performance. Let me just say that organizations that do not have 360 degree evaluations, suggestion boxes and or have a culture in which mistakes are punishable by career beheading, are usually organizations which also encourage or have a bully format imbedded.

Whatever the reason an asshole bullies, you can expect to see the following more subtle behaviors from the OB. They are usually inflexible and controlling. They deny information. They devalue others in both word and deed. The agendas are almost always theirs when dealing with either the target or subordinates in general. They have a posse or click of people who are generally homogenous to them in look, attitude and or behaviors. Favorites and pets. This behavior can also create a mob mentality as other who do not want the bully to focus and target them will side with them or remain silent when they see the behaviors being acted out on others.

OBs are usually smart, manipulative and crafty. They are generally petty, overbearing and hypercritical. They almost never take responsibility for their behaviors and often work to prove why others are to blame. They will also blame the person they are bullying for their behaviors by saying that the target brought it on. They don't solicit feedback about their behaviors, especially from those subordinates who are different in some meaningful way from them.

They will take credit for the work of others, often by answering questions from information obtained from the very people they target. They use manipulation ("born in vice, say it twice" {*King, 2001*}) and coercion as they do not work to build and sustain relationships. They will humiliate, undermine and even make fun of others to make themselves look good all the while calling their behavior politics or just having fun. They are usually afflicted with envy and jealousy. "Bullying is offensive, intimidating, malicious or humiliating behavior; abuse of power or authority which attempts to undermine an individual or group of employees and which may cause them to suffer stress." (*Peyton, 2003*).

This begs the question, once more, why we tolerate them within and outside of the workplace. I don't believe we should tolerate these behaviors. Yet, I do believe we should learn how not to behave this way ourselves. There really is no strong argument for allowing this behavior. It is imperative that we learn how to increase our Emotional Intelligence (EI) through study and practice, so that we do not do unto others what assholes have done to us.

Let me show you how I visualize EI paradigm. Look out when I start using big words.

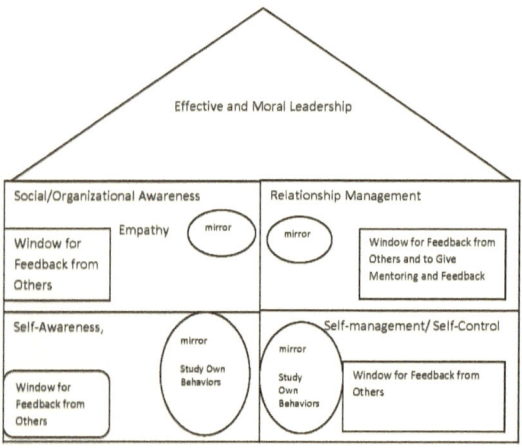

EI, Emotional Intelligence is a house with its foundations in self-awareness and self-management. The mirrors are larger in the foundation so that the person begins to look at their own behaviors, taking responsibility for the good and bad. This is where you and I begin to study how we behave and receive some feedback from others on how our behaviors are affecting them. For the other two building blocks you will have to invite me over to your porch to cover as it is imperative that you master the first two before building the rest of the house. Just remember, you cannot build a house without a solid foundation and expect it not to crumble at any storm. Don't believe me? Wait until the big bad wolf comes to huff and puff.

What I want to share next comes from Dr. Marsha Linehan's cognitive behavior advancements. She discussed the need to radically accept the things that you cannot change, like other people. She encourages being responsible for working on you and accepting the fact that life is not always fair. EI works on you experiencing your own feelings and emotions, while cognitive behaviors work on how you choose to act despite or because of your emotions. You need to do what is healthy for you and others. You also can work on being mindful of how both sides of your brain can work together to help you make wise choices in your behaviors, changes to your behaviors and how to give your boundaries; while listening for and showing respect for the boundaries of all others. Please remember that perceptions may be a reality to you or others, but facts are usually the what, when, where and how.

Well as we found on the front porch, I couldn't make a solid case for assholes in the workplace; however, it is clear that we do not want to become the OB in the workplace or any other place. We want to recognize such behaviors in ourselves. We also want to have the strength to guard against bullying by giving assholes clear unmovable boundaries. Absolutely no one has the right or privilege to belittle, devalue, manipulate, coerce or dehumanize you. And you do not have the right to do it to others. Whether someone has a title or not, does not mean they should be able to do so.

Most biblica make remarks on the subject of self-awareness and conduct toward others. Buddha has a chapter on awareness in the *Dhamma Pada*. I want to share some of it with you. It is also on your reading list. "The path to the Deathless is awareness; Unawareness, the path of death. They who are aware do not die; they who are unaware are as dead. Having known this distinctly, Those who are wise in awareness, Rejoice in awareness, Delighted in the pasture of the noble ones."

Confucianism speaks to living by the "golden mean," or being a virtuous person: A culture of "wen" in which we model good behavior and morality for people to follow. Dhyani Ywahoo the author of *Voices of Our Ancestors* gave us wisdom from the Cherokee when she spoke of "being responsible for kindling the fire of clear mind and right relationships." She charged us "have the courage and compassion to walk the Beauty Path to benefit all beings." The *Qur'an* expects us to make it our duty to, "seek the path of goodness, kindness, upright conduct and charity. To grasp at no advantage from a person's need. To stand by the word that is pledged, to bear true witness and remove all cause of misunderstandings." Don't make me pull out the *Bible* and the "fleck in our neighbor's eye while we have a log in our own . . ." thing. But, since I love Proverbs; "The king's heart is in the hand of the Lord, as the rivers of water: he turneth in whithersoever he will. Every way of a man is right in his own eyes: but the Lord pondereth the hearts. To do justice and judgment is more acceptable to the Lord than sacrifice."

Let's look at some language that may be helpful for you to use and encourage your staff to use when anyone, including you and your staff, are practicing bullying in the workplace. First, wait until you calm down and are aware of your feelings and the emotions being invoked by those feelings. Ask to voice your concerns. Be clear and direct about your concerns, how specific actions, behaviors or situations elicited feelings. Describe your feelings and offer suggestions of how you would like to be approached in the future. Try not to make assumptions, and ask questions to clarify the other person's perspective. Remember, feedback is a two way street and meant to offer positive outcomes, while criticism is a one way street where only one person talks without taking in the true needs, diversity and concerns of the other person.

Admit your shortcomings and take responsibility for the part you play in the relationship. Listen, respectfully when the other person is speaking. This one is difficult, but try to accept that others have a right to their perception and opinion just like we do. Remember, we are not always right either. In fact, the goal is not to be right, but to be heard and understood. Also, work on the courage to admit when the communication and trust are too fractured to be healed.

I can be real with you right? I mean, we have shared so much already. The one thing I have not done was take this to a more moral, and yes, spiritual level. *The Four Agreements*, puts what I am about to say a little bit differently and I want you to know that your religious affiliation is awesome with me as long has you practice the behaviors of doing well by others. So let's get to it. Most people are what I call drama junkies, me included. It really is about all of the things we were told about ourselves and more importantly what we have come to believe.

Freud worked from the premise that the id, ego and superego were often at odds with one another. The *Four Agreements* places this same scenario a bit differently and I am going to give you my version to take to the workplace. We all have a bully, self-image and a wounded child within. The bully (superego) in our heads puts us down, is hypercritical and tells us that we don't measure up. Our self-image (ego) struggles to deal with the judgments made about us from within ourselves and those judgments made by others. Our self-image also works to keep our impulses in balance. The wounded child (id) is that part of us which cringes every time we have to face the many fears we have because it operates from natural instinct. Fear of failure, fear of not being good enough, fear of being hurt one more time by people who are supposed to care for us.

We have to start to work on our fears and face them one by one. This is a hard task and a necessary one if we want to be the best we can each day. This is not something that we do overnight, nevertheless we must start by being honest about our fears and the actions we take against ourselves and others because of them.

My ten year old daughter ran for representative for the second grade, because she wanted to stop the bullying she experienced in school and she wanted to be honest about the pain and the behaviors she acted out because of her fears. She stood in front of her entire school and gave an awesome speech. Her, teacher, having a heart for her, told her during practice that her speech was wonderful, but that some of the kids might laugh at her admission of pain, fear and retaliation. As it turns out, no one laughed. All of the children in eight grades applauded her and each teacher and the principle came up to her to tell her how awesome she is and what a great rep she would be. In fact, the school decided that day to put a special group together to combat bullying.

The fact that I am gushing with pride and adoration notwithstanding, my daughter, my son and I had long conversations about this very issue over the years and more intensely in the days leading up to her powerful speech.

The morning of the speech she told me that she did not believe she had the courage that she saw in me to deliver the speech. I told her that I have been told that I appear fearless many times by others. However, the truth is that I have OCD as a result of childhood damage intensified by a fear of not being good enough and often being rejected. I told her that I am afraid much of the time and that courage does not mean that any of us is without fear. What it means to me, is that despite my fears, I do what should be done, what must be done, even afraid.

I raised two awesome children as a single parent. I put myself through school twice. I walked away from relationships and began again. I faced the most frightful demons; you know the ones in my own head and of my own making and even faced the demons of others. I have done all of this and much more afraid. I need each of you on the front porch to know that I believe that you can do the same.

I want you to find that wounded child within, pick them up and hold them. I want you to know that you are worthy and deserving of love, honor, dignity, kindness and peace as a right in your workplace. I want you to start by loving that wounded child and then the adult that, that child has become and have the courage to embrace who you are, your uniqueness and awesome qualities as well as your faults. Once you can do so, being honest about your fears and your behaviors, you can begin to heal. You will not allow anyone to bully you, even the bully in your head, and you will stop yourself from doing the same bullying to others.

It is clear that bullies hold a mirror to our own behaviors. They also encourage us to be responsible for our actions, work with integrity, live courageously and choose "what not to wear." I know you feel me and I know you can do this, besides we have a strict "no asshole behaviors," on the front porch. Like my grandmamma used to say, "child, don't make me come down off this porch."

Oh yeah, Job was bullied, and he questioned God, but never cursed God and he never bullied anyone else despite what was done to him.

Chapter Ten

Needed Information

I want to give you some needed information in the form of advice that you can choose to use or not as you see fit. You know your organization, colleagues, bosses, staff and customers (stake holders) best. However, I would encourage you to consider my advice in this chapter. There may be some useful information for you.

Mentorship—You need a mentor. The person does not have to be older, more formally educated or taller or anything like that. It does not even need to be someone you know that well. A mentor usually knows or has an understanding of situations, people and business that you do not. You would be asking them to work with you on building a better understanding of things. For instance, I did not understand our company's money end, so I asked two of the finance gurus to help enlighten me.

You can have several mentors depending on what you need to gain knowledge in. One type of mentor that is a must is someone, or several people, who can tell you the truth about your bad behaviors. You need to be able to trust that they have your best interest at heart and will not use what you share for anything other than your growth and redirection. Two of my organizational mentors are very similar in that they welcome debate and honesty from all members of the team. They don't take it as a personal affront when others don't agree with them; and they will willingly mentor others despite the impact on their already crazy schedules.

I have several mentors and most of them I trust to tell me the ugly things I don't like looking at about myself. You need this too as some of your behaviors are not stellar because you are human. You need to get in the practice of being able to understand how your behaviors are affecting your environment. Hence, some of those behaviors you may want to consider owning up to and changing. I'm just saying.

On the other hand, you need to be willing to provide mentorship to others as well. Remember, everything someone tells you is between the two of you especially when you are expressly asked to keep it so. Be honest with those you are mentoring, but understanding to their needs.

Encourage the Talent of Your People—I had an awesome boss named Sharon when I worked in Neonatal ICU and Concentrated Care Pediatrics. She took stock in my presentation and writing skills even back then, yes I was fly even back in the day, but nowhere near what I became under her tutelage. Sharon was confident and competent and so showed no petty insecurities. She was straight forward and recognized talent. She was unafraid to have intelligent staff who where experts. In fact, she wanted highly intelligent and talented nurses. She took pride in her nurse's achievements. She set us straight when she needed to, but she trusted that we would do our best. If we made a decision that went against a doctor, she would investigate, however she naturally assumed that her nurses were on top of their game unless they were proven to be otherwise.

She encouraged me to write a cultural diversity program for the staff. She taught me how to run staff and physician meetings. Because of her I was the first floor nurse to teach Pediatric Advanced Life Support for six years. She believed in me, despite my rough edges. I love Sharon.

Passion for Service—I have said this to a lot of people, leadership and supervision should be about providing excellent consumer service. Many managers and leaders believe that only their customers are their consumers and that they should only cater to their boss, or those people who look and or think like them. Actually, your consumer is everyone who is a stakeholder. One of your most important stakeholders is the people you lead and supervise. Your job is to ensure that they have everything that they need to do their job. This doesn't just mean office supplies. This means your time, mentorship, classes, education, and enough time to adequately plan and execute their job.

They need your trust, and understanding. They need you to hold them and yourself accountable. Providing them with the empowerment necessary to do their work and your humility are also important parts of your service as a leader and supervisor. Last, being upfront and honest with your team and being open to their honesty with you without punishing them for it in word or deed.

We can get so bogged down and overloaded with work that we can forget the importance of relationships. This has happened to me and I have seen it happen to others. When overloaded, I lose the passion and let go of relationships which can leave others seeing me as rude and uncompromising. I have to constantly remind myself that relationships and my passion for what I do are the two main reasons I go to work each day.

I am sure you don't ever want anyone to feel beat down and knuckled under either. I learned that I never want anyone to feel the way I did or others of my colleagues. I want people to know that I believe in mistakes as a foundation of learning. I truly care about people and want them to grow spiritually, personally and emotionally as well as professionally.

If no one can tell you that you are acting an ass, like my friend Tigger (nickname) does and you do not see it for yourself, then what? This is why we need to be a student of our own behaviors and we need to accept the mentorship of others. Remember the EI house that Luv built? There are mirrors in each room so that we remember to examine our behaviors.

There is a personality tool I use about every six months. I give it to my team and colleagues to see how they view me. I do one on myself too to see if what I think of my behaviors is what others are seeing too. It can be found online and it is the *Myers-Briggs Personality Types*. The trick to getting a true picture is to give this to at least eight or more people have them fill it out anonymously and don't just send to people you like and who like you. I learned a lot about my behavior from people who don't care for me.

Trust—Trust is earned and it is the foundation to all relationships. If you want to influence people you will need to have credibility. To have credibility you must demonstrate integrity. Integrity is when what you say matches up with what you do. I know a lot of people and I have done a lot of study on behaviors and psychology. Now I am no doctor, but here is what I have found to be true. You can tell within nine weeks to twelve weeks of knowing most people who they are. This is because people are what they do.

Remember, the first time you see some bad behavior; it could be an isolated incidence. The second time you see the same or similar behavior, it could be a coincidence. The third, fourth, fifth and so on time is called a behavioral pattern. Hey, you could even let the third time slide if you understand the person and their internal motivations, but beyond that . . .

Choosing to Change—I will tell you that you and anyone else can change what they are by changing their behaviors and replacing them with different behaviors. I know some notorious gossipers. In fact I have the awful distinction of being a recovering gossip junkie myself. I still slip and slide, however the way that I changed to behave better was to have only one or two people that I vent to and when others are venting I look for something good to say about the person they are talking about. If, in my heart I agree with what is being said, I start singing the hand washing song in my head to tune them out and then answer with, 'yeah, but they have a good heart.'
Let me say too, though people tell far out stuff like I am a change agent, you nor I can change anyone. I can only choose to change myself. Others may choose to change due to the effects of your behaviors in a given environment but the choice to make that change is up to them.

Building Sustainable Relationships—Building a relationship should mean that you grow to care for the other person. The relationship should have a foundation of trust. Trust is earned by consistently displaying integrity. Humans are social beings, for the most part. We want to know that other people genuinely care for and about us; not just giving lip service to get what we need out of them.

A word on encouraging a fun and just work environment. Okay, more than a word. I put this in relationships, because it is important. Think about those people, friends and family you have great relationships with, don't you have a good time with them? Why can't work be the same? I have found that people are far more productive, motivated and even delighted to be at work when their environment is fun, and I will say it, because I have been called weird, weird. We spend way too much time at work to be tribeless. I love working with my team and my friends. We spend a lot of our time laughing our canuties off and having people shh us, which makes us laugh even harder. You can always find us in the back pew at functions, and at the same table at meetings. And dear God, do not forget the jokes.

I work hard on establishing and developing trusting relationships. I have learned to listen to concerns and encourage fellow tribers and aspiring tribes. Therefore, I have the honor of having a relationship with some phenomenal people. An example is my friend Nanette McNamara who is a once in a lifetime boss. She is an expert at building relationships. When I started in my current work environment as a nurse, Nanette welcomed me into her tribe. She took me under her wing and offered me much needed mentorship and direction. She accepted me where I was emotionally and gently guided me to be able to trust by trusting in me. She invested in me. Nanette, let me know when I was off and made me tow the line, and when she chose to leave for her own reasons, it took me years to recover. I miss her even now.

Tribers—Your tribe is your posse. A part of your reading list is *Tribal Leadership*. You need to develop strong ties and real relationships with groups of people, not necessarily like minded in that you want people in the tribe to be diverse in their thinking. You want people who believe in similar core values. You also want to help people see the value in being genuine, trustworthy, loyal, caring, humorous, giving, fun, sharing, mistake makers, out of the boxers, make it happeners, relationship oriented, service driven, excellent, open minded, listeners who practice magic every day. You want your tribe members to be front porchers.

Let me share with you a place of wonder, tucked in between misted mountains, where the sun peeps through the vale to kiss all below. There is the faint smell of salt and the slight tingle of sea in the air. The building that houses this phenom and its magical people bears the look of the small hospital it once was. I cannot tell the name for fear that it might only have been some whispered half memory, but I know that I love it there. I love the people, the staff, the management and the leadership. The leader is CC and like all of her kind she is brilliant, open to ideas, creative and a student of her own behaviors. She loves a good argument and will accept one from all comers. She has a part of her team an arch of seven angels, her second named "Angel," in fact.

Her staff adores her and the organization has the highest productivity with the least outside support. Each member of the staff and it is hard to tell who is who as they often each lunch all together, is treated with respect, dignity and honored for their uniqueness and contributions to the whole. In all of my time spent coming in to offer paltry support, I have never heard one person mark another. I have detected no bully in their midst as they are designed against such assault by their leader. I have only seen its like twice before, once years ago as a new nurse working for a county hospital in the nursery; and once more in a dream called Camelot.

Be good to and show appreciation and understanding to your people; and they will be good to you. Spread your wings to take your team under them.

Taking Great Care of You—I cannot stress enough that you take great care of yourself, giving yourself daily breaks, good nutrition, exercise (which I am not fond of), proper uninterrupted sleep and the support of good friends and family. For those who are spiritual spending time in meditation and holy writ reading is also fundamental.

More to Talk About on the Next Visit to the Front Porch

Listen, I have had fun, but there is some stuff I need to take care of in the house, but maybe we can hang out again in the next book. Maybe next time we can spend more time on organizational cultures and subcultures. Maybe, we can blow out my favorite subject emotional intelligence.

A good leader has learned the fundamentals of leadership, wisdom, building relationships and mentoring. They have also come to understand the importance of studying and managing their own behaviors and emotions. They are accountable for their behaviors, hold others accountable for their behaviors and a good leader takes responsibility for ill results, while sharing the outcome of good results with their team. A great leader does all of this, but is necessarily an effective project manager. In this session of the front porch we are working with mentoring you to become a good leader one relationship at a time. When your organization or group invites us out we can help mentor you into great leadership.

I think I have bent your ear enough, just remember my favorite song from Charlie and the Chocolate Factory and what Kermit the Frog said, "it's not easy being green."
Ooh, hold on I almost forgot my book suggestions, you can find them online and in some brick and mortar stores:

Developing the Leader Within You
The 21 Irrefutable Laws of Leadership
The Happiness Hypothesis
Good to Great
Tribal Leadership
The Three Laws of Performance
Bad Bosses, Crazy Coworkers
Delivering Happiness
Dignity at Work
Work Place Bullying (What it is and What to Do About It)
The No Asshole Rule
Emotional Intelligence for Project Managers
The Leadership Test
The Four Agreements
Motivating Your Staff for Better Performance
King James Version (Bible)
Dhamma Pada (Buddhism)
The Voices of Our Ancestors
Logic for Dummies
Thomas More Source Book
The Prince and Other Writings
Managing Yourself
The Novelty of Leadership from the Front Porch (I know another shameless plug, tell a friend)

Bibliography

Daniel, M. (2000). *Emotional Intelligence Tests*. Toronto, Canada: Sterling Publishing.

Serebriakoff, V. (2000). *Emotional Intelligence Tests*. Toronto, Canada: Sterling Publishing.

Goleman, D. (1995). *Emotional Intelligence*. New York: Bantam Dell.

Mcshane, S. L. (2005). *Organizational Behavior, Emerging Realities for the Workplace Revolution* (Vol. 1, 3erd ed.). New York: McGraw-Hill/Irwin.

Von Glinow, M. (2005). *Organizational Behavior, Emerging Realities for the Workplace Revolution* (Vol. 1, 3erd ed.). New York: McGraw-Hill/Irwin.

Mcshane, Von Glinow, M. (2005). *Organizational Behavior, Mcgraw/ Hill Higher Education Website* (Vol. 1, 3erd ed.). New York: McGraw-Hill/Irwin.

Wagner, C. C. (2006). *Educational Psychology*. The College Network.

Cohen J., & Wagner, C. C. (2002). *Abnormal Psychology*. The College Network.

Mischel, W. (1999). *Introduction to Personality* (Vol. 1, 6th ed.). Harcourt Brace.

Kail, R. (2004). *Children and Their Development* (Vol. 1, 3rd ed.). Pearson Education Inc.

Turecki, S. (2000). *The Difficult Child* (2nd ed.). New York: Bantam.

Liker, Jeffrey. *Perspectives on Technology and Work Organization*. 1999. 575-96.

Byrne, Edmund. *Displaced Workers: America's Unpaid Dept.* 1985. 31-41.

Fallick, Bruce. *A Review of the Recent Empirical Literature on Displaced Workers*. 1996. 5-16.

Stout, PhD, Martha. *The Sociopath Next Door*. 2005.

Peyton, Pauline R. *Dignity at Work*. New York: Brunner-Routledge, 2003.

Linehan, PhD, Marsha. *Treating Borderline Personality Disorder*. 1993.